CW00547223

2 WILLOW ROAD
HAMPSTEAD

ALAN POWERS

The National Trust

Growing up at Willow Road
by Peter Goldfinger

I was between five and six years old when the three houses were being built. I have a vague memory of the excitement of the topping-out ceremony. My sister Liz was two or three.

No sooner had the family and servants (cook, au pair and chauffeur) moved into No.2, than war broke out. The rear of the garden level was turned into an air-raid shelter. The memory of a nightmare which turned out to be an air-raid warning remains with me. Then Liz and I were evacuated to Canada for the duration, returning in time for doodlebugs and V2 rockets and further use of that air-raid shelter. When our brother Mike was born in 1945, the Nursery rooms were full.

Meals were prepared in the ground-floor Kitchen and hoisted to the Dining Room Servery on the first floor by the dumb-waiter, which was manually operated by pulling on rather coarse hemp ropes. One of the maintenance chores, every two or three years, was to tension the rope balustrade of the circular stairs.

There were always people staying in the guest room on the second floor. These varied from near and distant relatives to a Swiss banker and a young female Italian film director. Some were paying guests, some came to stay for a couple of weeks and remained for over a year.

There was also a lot of entertaining. This ranged from quite small lunch and dinner parties and family meals to large cocktail parties, which involved opening up the folding walls on the first floor. Most guests seemed to be architects, many of them French friends from my parents' pre-war Paris days.

The internal arrangement of the house changed to accommodate the changing shape of the family. After we three children had moved out, Ernö's mother, Regine, moved in to two-thirds of the Nursery, with her amazing Austro-Hungarian furniture. We two married sons, at different times, lived in the flat that was created on the ground and garden floors. The Kitchen moved up to the Servery, and Ursula continued to produce wonderful meals from this tiny room. At one time there were four generations of Goldfingers living in the house – Regine (known as Little Granny, to differentiate her from Ursula), Ernö and Ursula, Mike and his wife, and their three sons. Time moved on. The downstairs flat was let. Little Granny died, aged 101. Both Ernö and Ursula died at home.

For me, one of the lasting memories and legacies of living at No.2 is an appreciation of art and architecture – accepting good modern work as the norm.

Ursula Goldfinger (centre) with her son Michael and sister-in-law Herta Goldfinger in the Dining Room around 1951

Ernö Goldfinger with his parents, Regine and Oscar, and his three children, Liz, Peter and Michael, on the first-floor terrace around 1946

Ernö Goldfinger and his mother Regine in the 1960s in her room at 2 Willow Road with its Austro-Hungarian furniture

Ernö and Ursula Goldfinger
The Early Years

Ursula Blackwell.
Photograph by Man Ray,
1939 (Living Room)

2 Willow Road was the home of the architect Ernö Goldfinger, his wife Ursula and their three children. When the house was completed in 1939, Goldfinger was 37 years old and had been living and working in London for five years. He was born in Budapest in 1902 and spent some of his early years among the forests of Transylvania where his father, a lawyer by profession, managed family saw-mills. He was educated in Budapest during the First World War, after which their land was taken into the newly created state of Romania.

In 1920 Goldfinger went to Paris, where he stayed with a cousin and learnt French, although his spelling was never very good. He had considered becoming a sculptor, but chose architecture instead and joined the atelier of Léon Jaussely at the Ecole des Beaux-Arts in 1921. The training was conservative, and in 1925 he joined with other students in persuading Auguste Perret, the master of reinforced concrete design, to set up a more progressive studio in a timber building of his own design in the Bois de Boulogne. This did not please the professors of the Ecole but Goldfinger preferred the company of the avant garde in architecture and art, many of whom he met through his cousin. He set up a partnership in 1929, a year before achieving his diploma, and designed some bare and stylish interior conversions for the lawyer Suzanne Blum, the painter Richard Wyndham, and other progressive clients. His first building, an extension to a holiday house in Le Touquet, was completed in 1933. In 1927 Goldfinger made his first visit to England to design a salon for Helena Rubinstein in Mayfair

and was impressed by the simplicity of Georgian buildings in London.

In 1931 Ernö Goldfinger met a young English woman, Ursula Blackwell, whom he persuaded to become a student of the Purist painter Amédée Ozenfant. Born in 1909 into a family that had made its money from Crosse & Blackwell soups, she was tall, slim and athletic, with a high forehead. Ernö's friend, the designer Charlotte Perriand, described her as 'a little distant, but friendly and observant'. He began designing a studio and house for her, which was evidently seen in their minds as a home for both of them. It was also meant to show the Blackwell family his own worth and to educate Ursula and the rest of the world in a superior way of living, free from false traditions and ideas. 'Goodness, love, art; they are in our heart and in us, and they will not be satisfied by little shows of propaganda', he wrote in 1931. The same letter goes on

Goldfinger's student card at the Ecole des Beaux Arts, Paris, 1927

Office for Maître Suzanne Blum,
Paris, 1930, with furniture by
Goldfinger

Design for 'The Outlook', Cucq,
Le Touquet, 1933, showing the
evolution of Goldfinger's ideas
of space and furniture in his first
executed building. The end wall
is bright red. Furniture includes
Goldfinger's 'Safari' chairs,
designed in 1929

to reveal that the Blackwells expected him to
build a house in Paris if they were going to get
married, but he explained to Ursula that he did
not yet want to be tied down:

*You know what importance I attach to building my
first house, and one specially for you, but one must*
know how to lose battles. We must think seriously
how to conceive this house so that it does not become
a weight which one drags after one for years or a
chain that attaches us to one place.

The house at Willow Road was a fulfilment of
this dream.

Paris in the Twenties

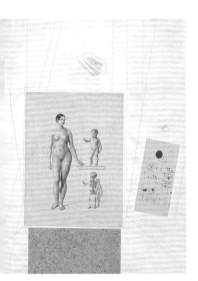

Max Ernst, *Loplop Présente (Facilité)*, collage and pencil on paper, 1931. One of a series of works by a leading artist of the Dada and Surrealist movements and friend of the Goldfingers featuring a bird-like *alter ego*. Bought for £25 in 1934

Charlotte Perriand wrote in 1983 of 2 Willow Road: 'It is an emotional experience staying there, surrounded by friendship, and by objects, books and pictures which recall the spirit of that unique epoch, for it was the birthplace of modern times.' She was referring to Paris in the 1920s, a period when the city attracted new thought in the arts from people of many nations. The Dada movement of the early 1920s was the exemplar for iconoclastic opposition, led by Marcel Duchamp, Max Ernst and Hans Arp (whose work can be seen at Willow Road), but other groups also embraced risk and danger in search of truth.

In 1925 Goldfinger was at the centre of an attempt to change architectural education in Paris. As he described it:

At the Beaux-Arts everything was dead. All this stirring of modern architecture was ridiculed... We weighed up whether we should ask [the Swiss] Le Corbusier or Perret to teach us architecture. It was [the Moravian-Viennese architect and theorist] Adolf Loos who said: 'When you come to Paris you come to learn French not Esperanto.'

Perret based his theory and designs on the French tradition of 'structural rationalism', a doctrine that combined Gothic and classical

Ernö Goldfinger (standing with hat) at the Café du Dôme, Paris, a meeting-place of artists and intellectuals. Photograph by André Kertész

sources in looking for the essentials of architecture. He was also one of the first architects to treat reinforced concrete in an artistic manner. Goldfinger revered the memory of Perret, and his influence is apparent at Willow Road, particularly in the compact geometry of the spiral staircase and in the concrete columns, which were formed in shuttering that suggests classical fluting, and exposed as objects of beauty in themselves.

Loos developed a theory of domestic planning known as the *Raumplan* ('space plan'). This was a modification of open planning which conceived a house as a series of volumes fitted into a plain exterior envelope. Although rooms were no longer to be compartmented in the 19th-century sense, they were made distinctive in character and use by changes in level and shape, particularly in height. Fitted furniture emphasised the architectural character of the interior. This was undoubtedly influential in Goldfinger's conception of Willow Road.

The relationship between architecture, art and life was axiomatic in the Paris of the '20s. Ursula Blackwell's teacher Amédée Ozenfant was a former collaborator of Le Corbusier and believed in the methodical study of fundamentals rather than the primacy of any particular style or movement. His book *Foundations of Modern Art* (French edition, 1929; English edition, 1931) emphasised the excitement of a liberated art, challenging the conventions of civilisation and absorbing ideas from anthropology, literature and contemporary life. The collection of ethnic objects at Willow Road mirrors Ozenfant's illustrations.

Some of the artists who became Goldfinger's friends, notably Max Ernst, S.W.

Hayter, Roland Penrose and Lee Miller, were associated with the Surrealist movement, founded in Paris in 1923 and committed to the liberation of the individual through delving into the subconscious. Surrealism spanned all the arts, but although it had no clear representation in architecture, many architects shared its heightened awareness of the emblematic quality of objects and its fondness for assaulting the public with polemic and propaganda.

Among the Surrealist devices reflected at Willow Road is the emphasis on framing openings. The Surrealists were also pioneers in the collecting and display of found objects, elevating things otherwise considered worthless into items of curiosity and inspiration. Although the early photographs of 2 Willow Road show relatively few objects, the Goldfingers had by the end of their lives accumulated a rich background for their collection of works of art.

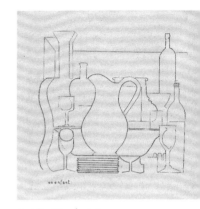

Amédée Ozenfant, *Fugue*, etching, 1925. The calm classicism of domestic objects exemplifies the Purist movement of Ozenfant and Le Corbusier

The framed screen in the Living Room is a Surrealist device and was used to display a changing collection of the Goldfingers' pictures

Max Ernst, *Pebble*, granite, 1934

Life in London

The Goldfingers were married in Paris in 1933, the year in which their son Peter was born. They moved to London in 1934 and Ernö set up an office in Bedford Square. In 1935 they took a three-year lease on a flat in Highpoint I, Highgate, the most elegant modern block in London, which had been designed by Ernö's rival, Berthold Lubetkin; their second child Elizabeth was born here. Michael, their third child, was born in 1945.

In his pre-war London years, Goldfinger designed many unbuilt projects. Apart from Willow Road, his only executed building was a house at Broxted in Essex for the painter Humphrey Waterfield. He occupied himself with other kinds of design, including furniture for his Highpoint flat. For the educational toy firm of Paul and Marjorie Abbatt, Goldfinger designed a shop front and showroom, toys and exhibition installations, including the Children's Section of the British Pavilion at the Paris Exhibition held in 1937.

Eileen Agar, *Ernö Goldfinger*, pen and ink on paper, 1938. The artist was one of the most imaginative of English Surrealists

Shop for S. Weiss, Golders Green Road, NW11. A conversion of an existing building by Goldfinger, 1935. The building survives with alterations

(*Right*) Entrance to Paul and Marjorie Abbatt's toy shop, 94 Wimpole Street, W1, 1936

Hampstead in the Thirties

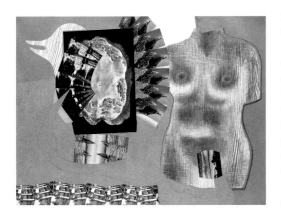

Nancy Cunard at the 'Aid to Russia' exhibition at 2 Willow Road. Picasso's *La Niçoise* hangs on the Living Room screen

During the 1930s Hampstead replaced Chelsea as the place where significant numbers of progressive artists and writers lived and worked. The attractive combination of relatively cheap property and the amenities of Hampstead Heath had drawn artists, architects and writers to the higher parts of Hampstead Village since the 19th century, but the formation of an informal arts colony in the lower parts, stretching over towards Belsize Park, reached its culmination at the time that Ernö Goldfinger was building 1–3 Willow Road. By the 1950s, 'Hampstead intellectual' had become a byword for left-wing idealism, probably cushioned by a good education and standard of living.

The critic Herbert Read spoke of his neighbours in the Mall Studios, Parkhill Road, as 'a gentle nest of artists'. These included Ben Nicholson, Barbara Hepworth and Henry Moore, who became Britain's best-known international artists after the Second World War. They represented the evangelical tendency to abstraction and were fittingly joined by two of the most important European artists in this field,

Piet Mondrian and Naum Gabo, who lived in Parkhill Road in the later 1930s.

The Modernist credentials of this corner of Hampstead were firmly established by the construction in 1934 of the Isokon Flats in Lawn Road, designed by the architect Wells Coates to a brief given by Jack Pritchard, a salesman for Venesta plywood, and his wife Molly, a psychiatrist. The flats were built of reinforced concrete and each was planned for economy of space, for a modern person living without many possessions. The Isobar, a club on the ground floor, opened in 1935, designed by F.R.S. Yorke and Marcel Breuer, one of many emigrés from Nazi Germany helped by the Pritchards. Despite the general financial hardship and political uncertainty of the time, the Pritchards created an atmosphere in which wit, ideas, and good food and drink flourished.

Not all the artists and architects in Hampstead necessarily knew each other, even if their work showed similar directions. Among the moderns and progressives there was an increasing division after 1936 between Surrealists and Abstractionists. However, both sets were politically left-wing, and Goldfinger was one of those who signed the manifesto of the English Surrealist group calling for the government to lift its arms embargo to Republican Spain during the Spanish Civil War. This political activism was manifested again in the exhibition held in 1942 at 2 Willow Road for the 'Aid to Russia' Fund of the National Council of Labour. Although many of the Hampstead artists had dispersed by this time to St Ives and other parts of rural England or to America, the exhibition showed work by Moore, Hepworth, Nicholson and Penrose.

(*Above*) Henry Moore, *Head*, elm and string, 1938. A small but important work by the leading British modern sculptor, who lived in Hampstead in the 1930s. Bought from the 'Aid to Russia' exhibition

(*Left*) Roland Penrose, *The Real Woman*, collage, pencil and watercolour on board, 1937. A gift from the artist, who was a friend from Paris days and lived at 21 Downshire Hill

One of Goldfinger's poster designs for the travelling exhibitions of the Army Bureau of Current Affairs

The Post-war Years

(*Above*) Goldfinger standing in front of Trellick Tower, North Kensington, a controversial 31-storey housing slab block of 1967

(*Below*) Alexander Fleming House, Elephant and Castle, 1962. A revival of the 'Heroic' modern architecture of the 1920s

In the post-war years Goldfinger was able to restart his practice with schools in Putney and Hammersmith, a small block of flats near Regent's Park, and some industrial buildings. In association with the developer Arnold Lee, Goldfinger designed a small office building in Albemarle Street, followed by the large office complex at Elephant and Castle for the Ministry of Health known as Alexander Fleming House.

Goldfinger had always wanted to design tall buildings, and two housing commissions from the GLC, which placed him on its approved list of 'outside' architects, enabled him to do so in the 1960s. The Rowlett Street scheme (1965) beside the north entrance to the Blackwall Tunnel included Balfron Tower, a 27-storey slab-block mainly of maisonettes. In 1967 the Goldfingers lived for two months at the top of this tower block as a demonstration of his confidence in the design. In the same year he began work on housing for

the Cheltenham Estate in North Kensington, including the similar but even taller Trellick Tower, about which he remained quite unapologetic when popular opinion turned sharply against such buildings. After these housing commissions were completed in 1973, he designed a small number of private houses and commercial interiors, closing his office in 1977.

In the post-war period Goldfinger did not achieve the success of some of his younger contemporaries and stayed slightly outside their clubbish circle, perhaps owing to his outspoken manner and his hard-edged and rational architecture. He was a man whose company was never dull, of whom great rages and great affection are remembered; he refused to grow old. When he died on 15 November 1987, James Dunnett, an architect who had worked on his later housing schemes, wrote; 'The greatest honour that can now be paid to him and his example is carefully to look after his work.'

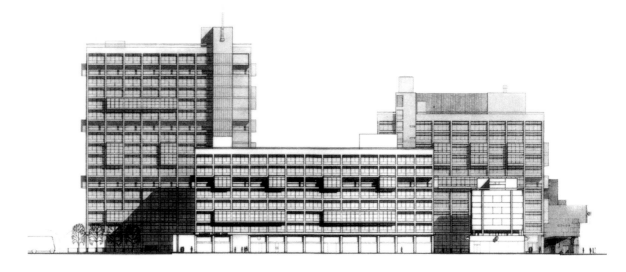

(*Right*) Ernö and Ursula Goldfinger in the Living Room at 2 Willow Road in his 81st year

1–3 Willow Road

Design and Construction

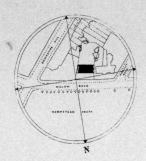

(*Above*) The site extends well back from the road

(*Below*) The previous buildings on the site, showing the fall in the land

The site near the junction of Willow Road and Downshire Hill was previously occupied by four small cottages set back and partly below the level of the road, flanked by the newly rebuilt Freemasons' Arms, a large neo-Georgian pub. It is nearly square in shape and faces a triangle of open land at the edge of Hampstead Heath, looking almost due north. Formerly belonging to the owner of 47 Downshire Hill, it had changed hands in 1935. When the Goldfingers became interested in the site, they saw it as a way of providing themselves with a place to live, investing some of Ursula's capital, and giving Ernö a chance to demonstrate his skill as an architect. Architects had fewer opportunities to design their own houses in the 1930s than after the war, and these were mostly in the country.

The first designs made for the site by Goldfinger in October 1936 were for a block of flats incorporating studios, appropriately facing north, one of which would have been for his own family. Among modern architects,

building flats was considered a more socially useful exercise than building individual houses, and Goldfinger had designed several studio spaces in Paris. Highpoint, where the Goldfingers were then living, had been conceived as an exercise in communal living, as had the nearby Isokon Flats. The scheme for flats enabled more of the site to be filled and was taken to a detailed design after several trial configurations, but this was rejected by the London County Council.

A design made in July 1937 shows four houses in a terrace, repeating the existing use of the site but bringing the building line closer to the road and dropping down internally to a lower garden level. By September something closer to the final design had been reached. Two sites were amalgamated in the centre of the terrace to make a larger house nearly square in plan, while the end houses had oblique end walls fitted to the shape of the site.

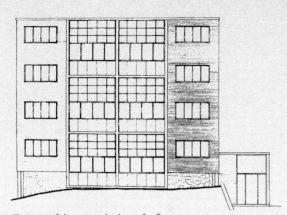

Elevation of the rejected scheme for flats

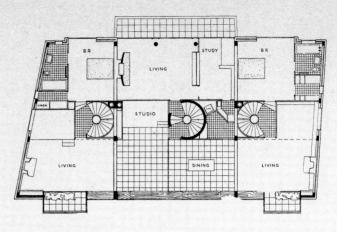

Plan of the first floor of 1–3 as built.
The terrace form neatly masks the angled boundaries

(*Above*) Dwelling functions are separated by levels in the section: nursery and bedroom above, living on the first floor, kitchen and maids' rooms on the ground floor, and laundry, garden room and boiler beneath. Although resembling a traditional terrace house arrangement, the large windows and flat roof enable the centre of the deep plan to be well lit

(*Right*) Perspective of 1–3 Willow Road. The left-hand house was rented by the Goldfingers to the classical scholar R.P. Winnington-Ingram. No.3, on the right, was pre-sold to Stephen Wilson, a civil servant, and completed to his specifications. The design of the elevations aims at a unified effect rather than a series of individual houses

Sketch for the Dining Room

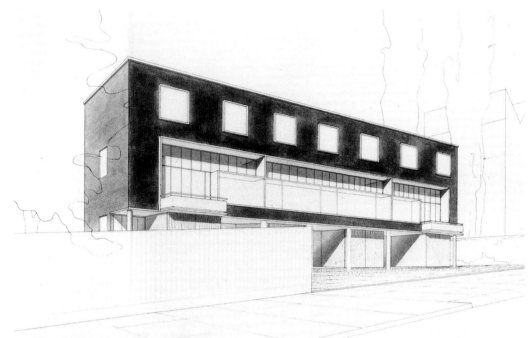

A considerable effort went into the design of all the houses to reconcile the demands of construction, space, social life and the controlling authorities. The concrete frame, relying on the cylindrical well of the spiral stair for additional strength, was calculated by structural engineers J.L. Kier & Co. The first floor of No.2 was designed as far as possible as a flexible space, and, although the possibility of a double-height studio was eliminated, the change in floor level in the centre of the house helped to separate the apparent functions. The end houses had L-shaped drawing rooms. The flat roof allowed for the staircase and bathrooms to be lit from above and buried in the centre of the plan, thus saving the window walls for the bedrooms and Nursery. Although the style was modern, the plans for No.2 included rooms for two living-in servants and, until a late stage, a tradesmen's entrance beside the front door. Modern amenities included two garages (one with an inspection pit) and two bathrooms.

Several alterations were made to the window design to satisfy the LCC, which stipulated a higher proportion of wall to window for reasons of fire protection. When the design was finally submitted to Hampstead Borough Council and the LCC at the end of 1937, a letter of protest to the local newspaper from Henry Brooke, Secretary of the Heath and Old

(*Above*) The topping-out ceremony with the Goldfinger family and building workers

(*Left*) During construction, the loadbearing concrete slab and columns were clearly visible at the rear of the house

Hampstead Protection Society and later MP for Hampstead, started a controversy that reached the national press in the ensuing weeks.

In defending his design, Goldfinger was concerned to emphasise its conformity to the surroundings and to the tradition of Georgian building in London. This was not special pleading, as he shared the admiration of many foreign architects for the simplicity and orderliness shown, for example, in the Regency villas in Downshire Hill, although ignored in the neighbouring late Victorian houses in Willow Road itself. He explained that very little concrete would be exposed to view and cited the modern concrete house at 13A Downshire Hill, which had been built by the architects Michael and Charlotte Bunney without protest three years before, concluding that 'only the Esquimeaux and Zulus build anything but rectangular houses'.

The contract for building 1–3 Willow Road was awarded to Leslie Bilsby, a young builder with a belief in modern architecture. The contract price for No.2 was £2,751 6s 1d and the total cost of the house and land on completion was £3,885. The actual client was a company, Contemporary Construction Ltd, formed to represent Ursula's investment interest. The houses were completed in the summer of 1939, shortly before the declaration of war on 3 September.

Architectural Analysis

An early photograph of the Living Room with the windows opened back

The terrace form of 1–3 Willow Road was determined by the conditions of the site and the opposition to building flats in Hampstead. When the completed project was published in the *Architectural Review* in 1940, it was prefaced by a two-page article, 'The Decline of the Street and an Attempt to restore it', defending the formality of street architecture, which had fallen out of favour with house-buyers and architects. It praised the 18th-century terraces where individual houses are subordinated to the composition of the whole. Willow Road was put forward as a model offering some choice in the house plans and elevations without loss of overall architectural coherence. In this respect, it was seen as corresponding to 18th-century values without imitating Georgian forms.

Concrete construction and continuous windows allowed for a greater level of daylight than in earlier terraces. By confining staircases and bathrooms to the core of the houses, the living rooms gain all the benefits of outlook. The main sitting rooms on the first floor return to the Georgian prototype of the *piano nobile* and allow for much of the ground floor to be occupied by garages.

Goldfinger was insistent on the need to give a visual termination to a modern façade, hence the stone coping course on the parapet, which also prevents weather-staining on the brick-work. This is a traditional detail that Modernists of the 1920s in Europe often omitted in the interests of geometric purity. Compared to the high maintenance needed for the 'white archi-tecture' of the 1930s in England, Willow Road has kept its appearance with no more effort than that required for a conventional house.

The Willow Road houses, looking out over Hampstead Heath with no other buildings in view, represent the ideal aim of modern archi-tecture to make the benefits of country life and holidays available in towns. The Goldfingers shared the enthusiasm of their generation for open-air activity. Large windows were one way of bringing indoor life closer to the regenerative forces of nature. Goldfinger was committed to the reform of the city according to the ideas of Le Corbusier, opening up green spaces and letting in sunlight.

The influence of Auguste Perret is evident in the concrete construction of 1–3 Willow Road. Perret developed the French Rationalist tradition, which valued the elegant expression of structure and the clear articulation of load-bearing members. Many English Modernist

houses of the 1930s had aspired to appear as complete concrete boxes, with walls and roof made as one piece of monolithic construction. At Willow Road, the floors, stairs and inner leaf of the walls are of concrete, with concrete columns bearing the floor slabs. On the street front the columns appear on the ground floor while the weight of the second floor is carried behind the wide window on thin steel stan-chions. The back of the building is more logi-cal, with two concrete columns running through from basement to second floor, slightly set back from the first-floor windows so that they can be seen in the round and leave space for a curtain track between columns and window.

The concrete structure of the house consists of roof and floor slabs linked by the stairwell and supported on columns at the edges

The main first-floor windows on the street front (*above*) are divided by a long concrete shelf just above head height, with the glass set back in the upper part. This 'photobolic screen' reflects light from its white-painted upper face on to the ceiling of the Dining Room and Studio (*above left*). The device was repeated in many Goldfinger buildings. In contrast to many modern houses of the 1930s, concrete is not a dominant material on the visible surfaces of the building

The Interior

The first floor thrown open by folding back all the partitions

Sketch for the Living Room

(*Right*) View from the Studio to the Living Room in 1940, showing the change in level

Inspired by the *Raumplan* theory of Adolf Loos, 1–3 Willow Road have a stepped cross-section on the first floor. This adds to the variety of the rooms and makes an attractive step down from the rear living room to the front. The consequence is a very low ceiling in the hall, but this encourages one to continue up the stairs. The spiral staircase serves both levels without requiring large landing spaces.

Movable partitions and folding doors are a feature on the first floor of No.2. The Studio can be opened into the Dining Room and the Living Room, although the partitions seem to have been kept shut most of the time during winter. In the early versions of the plan the Study was also divided by a foldaway screen from the Living Room.

The use of colour in modern houses of the 1930s is often forgotten, because they were only photographed in black and white, but it plays an important part at Willow Road. The three front doors in white, red and dark blue are the only indication from outside, but inside No.2 a carefully devised sequence of colours defines the surfaces of walls and floors and enhances the moods of the house. The colours selected and the way that they are used derive much from the experiments of Le Corbusier and Ozenfant in the 1920s, which in turn owed much to Cubist painting and its celebration of ordinary life. The palette of colours grows lighter and brighter as one rises through the house, and the range of colours is similar to those used by Cubist painters such as Georges Braque and Juan Gris. After Ernö's death, Ursula Goldfinger supervised the repainting of the interior, matching the original colours.

Texture also plays a part. Although most of the surfaces are smooth, they vary from the reflective shine of Armstrong tile floors and gloss paint to matt plywood and fine-textured concrete. In the early photographs a polar bear fur rug is shown on the Studio platform leading into the Living Room, giving a contrasting note of extreme softness – a juxtaposition often found in Surrealist paintings and constructions.

Services

The original ground-floor Kitchen in 1940. The simple sliding cupboard doors have no projecting handles and the drawers are pulled by a grooved lip at the base of the drawer-front. This kitchen was dismantled in the 1960s, when the ground floor became a separate flat

Modern architecture used the most advanced mechanical services available, but by the 1930s these had not developed very far. Heating was from a solid-fuel boiler in the basement, although this had a specially designed coal-hole accessible from the street. The radiators are conventional of their period in heavy cast iron. The Living Room has an open fire, a feature of nearly all modern houses of the 1930s in spite of its traditional associations, although here it is contained entirely within its opening, lifted off the floor to provide more effective radiant heat and prevent the clutter of a hearth.

Light fittings are as unobtrusive as possible. Goldfinger declared that most designers of lighting concentrated on the look of the object they were making rather than thinking about the kind of light it would provide. None the

less, the wall-mounted uplighters in the Dining Room, which were made to his own design, are elegant objects in themselves.

Bathroom fittings were selected from manufacturers' catalogues to be as geometrically pure as possible. The inclusion of a bidet in the master bathroom was rare for an English house at this time. A hand-operated dumb-waiter, as found in many older terraced houses, linked all the floors.

The guest bathroom in 1940. Neatness and simplicity

Furniture and Fittings

The clock, light switches and door handle in the Living Room were all fitted flush with the oak plywood walls

The Dining Room sideboard, showing the cutlery drawers

The bedroom cupboards conceal elaborate drawers and fittings, precisely matched to individual items of clothing. They also conform to the proportional system based on the square and the Golden Section and used throughout the design of the house

To preserve the sense of pure volumes within the house, built-in cupboards and fittings were provided wherever possible. Space is found in the thickness of the walls or in the partitions, where the cupboards also act as sound insulation. Some of the cupboards have 'tambour' fronts made of rounded wooden battens mounted on canvas that slide out of sight, a technique of traditional French cabinetmaking. The main bedroom wardrobe is fitted with wooden trays, each carefully dimensioned to particular articles of dress. In place of a conventional dressing-table, Ernö designed for Ursula a built-in fitting in the Bathroom with mirrored doors and a concealed light in the recess above.

Much of the door furniture was to Goldfinger's own designs. In the 1930s the production of small runs of craftsman-made objects was easier, although these were seen

as prototypes for future mass production. Light switches were carefully positioned for functional and visual effect. The attention to such very small details was also intended to achieve unity of style within a single building. The house is well provided with ledges and recesses. These are occupied by a variety of found objects and works of art which enhance the architectural quality of the interiors and refute the accusation of cold austerity often made against modern houses in the 1930s.

The built-in furniture relates in form and material to the movable furniture previously designed by Ernö Goldfinger for his Paris apartment and brought to Willow Road, as well as to pieces newly created for the house. His early work consisted largely of interiors, and the provision of fitted furniture extended into the design of special chairs, desks and tables. The 'Safari' chairs, of timber and leather, were adapted from a traditional demountable design first made for Lee Miller in Paris in 1927. The Richard Wyndham studio included a stylish desk with corner-pivot drawers.

Most modern architects designed furniture, some, like Le Corbusier, Mies van der Rohe and Alvar Aalto, producing classics that have remained in production. Goldfinger's friendship with Charlotte Perriand, collaborator with Le Corbusier in furniture, brought him into the innermost circle of modern design and he treated nearly all his furniture designs as prototypes for mass production, hoping that they might become a source of income. He was less fortunate with the generally conservative British makers and retailers, perhaps because his theories of comfort were sometimes at odds with experience, as with his pivoting chair-

backs. He did not always adapt his architectural outlook to the demands of materials, but he was original in using industrial objects and materials such as machine-tool bases for tables and sections of steel beam for supports. These pieces have a solid architectural quality like miniature monumental buildings. In accordance with the precepts of Adolf Loos, Goldfinger looked for high standards of craftsmanship that would make simple, impersonal forms appear beautiful. His principal commercial range was a set of storage units designed for Easiwork Ltd in 1938 using many tambour doors, as seen on pieces at Willow Road.

Liz Goldfinger designed a number of wooden chairs in the 1960s, of which examples are found at 2 Willow Road.

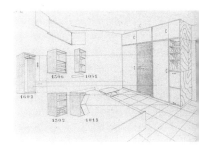

(*Above*) Goldfinger's designs for 'Easiwork' fitted cupboards, 1937

(*Below*) Pivoting drawers mounted on a table leg were a favourite Goldfinger device. This desk also has a narrow drawer within the desktop

23

Tour of the House

The Entrance Hall

The hall is a low-ceilinged space, lit by obscured glass flanking the front door, set into a grid of compartments in which objects can be displayed and one of which includes the letter slot with a hinged glass plate on the inside to stop the letters falling on the floor. The floor was originally of red ochre tiles; the present rubber stud flooring was installed in the 1970s. The walls are white and slate-blue, with a cork pin-board on the facing wall. In place of conventional skirting boards, a 'hospital skirting' is used here and throughout the house, carrying the floor surface up in a curve to merge with the wall. The door frames are made with a deeply projecting profile to allow for a neat termination of the skirting.

The low cabinet in waxed oak with double tambour doors is a Goldfinger design. On the

The Entrance Hall includes a prototype bent plywood chair by Goldfinger, painted in grey and red

right a narrow cloakroom with a sliding door is fitted within the space created by the curved outer wall of the stairwell. To save space, the cistern is on the other side of the wall in the former garage (now cinema). The door at the end of the hall originally led to a tiled lobby giving access to the service part of the house – two maid's bedrooms, the Kitchen and, reached by a smaller spiral staircase, the basement garden room and laundry. This was converted to a separate flat by the Goldfingers and occupied mostly by members of their family. It has been remade by the National Trust into a flat reached through the left-hand garage.

The Stairs

The concrete stairs are supported from the wall and bolted to a steel strap which leaves a central void as it rises. The brass handrail is braced by widely spaced steel supports, the intervening balustrade being formed of tensioned rope threaded between loops to create a zig-zag pattern. The bottom step is broader than the others to allow for an easier ascent. The stairwell is painted a warm grey, although originally described as beige.

The spiral stairs display great potential for effects of light and shadow. Photographed in 1940

The Dining Room

At the first turn of the stairs, a split-level landing offers three directions – to right and left and ahead: Living Room, Dining Room or Studio. The door, wall and ceiling surfaces of the two recesses off the stairwell are painted in bright red gloss. The Dining Room is entered on the line of the central axis of the house. It can be combined with the Studio by folding back the four-leaf floor-to-ceiling partition, which is hinged half from the wall and half from the window sides of the room.

Along the full extent of the north side of the house, the windows overlook Hampstead Heath, which was more open in the 1930s than now. A deep window-sill faced in plywood is carried over radiators and the outlook is framed by the lower ledge of the 'photobolic screen', above which are casement windows. The objects on the window-sill increased in number over the years. Mostly of wood, they include African carvings, utensils and a lay figure reclining in a model of a Goldfinger

The first floor with partition doors closed

A Goldfinger uplighter with ribbed glass industrial reflector shade

The Dining Room with Goldfinger's table and chairs

chair. For many years two pond yachts were placed here and visible from the street.

The Kitchen off the Dining Room was created from the original Servery when the basement flat was made.

The wall facing the windows is painted in terracotta red beneath a band of slate blue denoting the concrete structure, the end wall white. The floor is of dark grey-green tiles. Curtains were originally of green parachute silk. The present ones are a replacement using a textured natural coloured silk from France, of which an earlier set survives in the Studio.

The dining-chairs are made of chromed steel tubing with pressed plywood seats and pivoting backs, to a design by Ernö Goldfinger for his Highpoint flat. The dining table has a lino top, lipped with hardwood and glued to plywood, mounted on a cast-iron industrial machine-tool base. The table top is a wider replacement designed by Goldfinger when the sideboard was moved from the side to the end wall. Both pieces were originally made for Highpoint, the sideboard having behind its white sliding doors handsome cutlery drawers with inset ivory knobs. On the sideboard stand two florid electroplate candlesticks.

The Studio

While entered directly from the stairs, the Studio can be merged with the Dining Room and Living Room, from which it is separated by a folding partition faced in gaboon mahogany, with the Living Room side faced in oak. The end leaf nearest the stairs acts as a door in line with the two steps inset in the wooden platform, which is a continuation of the Living Room floor. The platform is lit to act as a

model stand and is fitted with plan-chest drawers. Storage cupboards for pictures and materials are provided in the wall. Although the Studio was the constant element through all stages of the design development of the house, Ursula seems never to have had time to make full use of it for her painting.

The bookcases in the lower part of the Studio were heavily laden and the floor space almost completely taken over when Goldfinger closed his architectural office in 1977 and transferred some of its contents to Willow Road, including the black laminate-top desk, which has pivoting drawers on both sides.

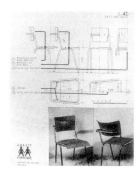

A miniature version of the Dining Room chairs designed for Paul and Marjorie Abbatt

The Studio with Goldfinger's office desk and chair. Steel columns take the place of concrete to give maximum outlook

The Living Room

This room was the subject of many alternative designs, worked into elegant and dreamlike perspective sketches. It can be reached either from the Studio or directly from the upper stair-well. With the Studio partition closed, it is a light but intimate space looking over the back gardens of Downshire Hill. Two smoothly painted concrete columns stand clear of the hinged timber glazing, which can be folded outwards to give clear access to the balcony either side of the central column. The double curtain track between windows and columns carries sun curtains and heavier silk curtains.

The fireplace is formed from a convex screen-wall running from floor to ceiling, into which the dark steel frame of the fire opening is inserted to clear the ground. There is a decorative cast-iron fireback of a salamander, introducing a baroque note matched in the Staffordshire watch-stand figure group on the ledge above. A green marble hearthstone is laid flush with the parquet flooring. The wings of the screen wall are clear of the back wall and the lighting was originally concealed behind these, later being replaced by hinged bracket-mounted uplighters.

The wall surfaces are faced in waxed oak plywood. Opposite the fireplace a projecting wooden frame, bevelled at the edge on the inner face, was built for the display of paintings and objects. It also contains the projection of a bookshelf and cupboard unit in the Study beyond, which had been removed from the Goldfingers' Paris flat for reuse. By the door from the stairs, the clock mounted low in the wall is a type used in aircraft which can be wound by turning the milled outer ring. Beside this are single light switches and a bell-push inserted in vertical alignment into the wooden wall-covering without any fingerplates.

The Study

This small room is fitted with one complete wall of bookshelves containing much of Goldfinger's working library, travel books and a copy of Ian Fleming's *Goldfinger*, according to legend named after Ernö. Books and magazines with articles by or about himself are marked with red labels. The low-crowned grey top hat belonged to Auguste Perret. In metal filing cabinets and drawers Goldfinger kept his extensive collection of photographs and slides.

A door (now blocked) in the blue-grey painted wall originally gave access to the darkroom, which was later incorporated in the first-floor Kitchen.

The Study with its important collection of architectural books

Goldfinger's 1977 perspective of the Studio and Living Room

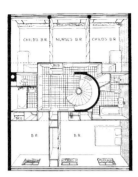

The second floor. Cupboards are built into the partitions and help to vary the room shapes

The Top Landing is flooded with light from above

The Top Landing

The stair terminates beneath a circular rooflight in a landing with blue painted walls and Armstrong tile floor in buff yellow. Two doors at the head of the stairs lead to the second bathroom and separate WC, between which hangs a brightly coloured oriental mask.

The separation of the rooms from the landing by a cupboard zone adds some attractive spatial qualities to this floor. Set back within this zone are doors leading to the Nursery to allow for its division with partitions into separate bedrooms for two children and a nurse (or nanny) in the centre. The end door is set slightly mysteriously out of sight behind the outer face of the stairwell, lit by day through an opening with vertical fin-shaped slats, providing in turn a source of concealed electric light at night. This space, which was later shut off to form a broom cupboard, also contained the dumb-waiter, which brought food up from the Kitchen two floors below.

The Main Bedroom

Entered immediately to the left at the head of the stairs, the main bedroom occupies two bays of the north side of the house, at this level demarcated by square windows whose external framing in stone is reflected in the internal oak linings carried round all four sides. The white laminate sills were a later modification. The room is not large, but the apparent space is increased by the low level of the simple bed. Goldfinger believed that the higher civilisations, such as the Japanese, slept closer to the ground. Bookshelves beside the bed are braced against floor and ceiling with telescopic poles. Lighting is provided by Goldfinger's uplighters and wall-mounted angle-poise bedside lights. Clothes

The austere Main Bedroom with bathroom beyond

were stored in the elaborately fitted cupboards opposite the bed and along the side wall, both with luggage lockers overhead. One wall was originally distempered duck-egg blue; all are now white.

The Bathroom

A door leads to a bathroom top-lit by a circular skylight. The low soffit over the door is painted slate-blue gloss and this colour is carried down the wall. The curved outer face of the stairwell carries a curved towel rail. The basin is Goldfinger's replacement of the original, conforming to his requirement for a square overall shape bracketed clear of the wall. Two doors with chrome knobs open to reveal a vanity unit with its own internal lighting and glass shelves to both sides. In the narrower part of the room the colour scheme is continued with the scarlet-painted shelf recess and a slate-blue below. A sliding door leads to the WC with its own skylight.

The Spare Bedroom

The cupboard zone backing on to the second bathroom allows space for a narrow tip-up bed to be concealed, with its own overhead light in a metal box reflector. To the right is a wash-basin concealed in a cupboard. The main bedroom cupboards provide acoustic separation, the spare room having two narrow tambour-fronted storage units, reused from the Goldfingers' Paris flat, in the left-over space. A flash of bright red runs up beside the door.

The wall as service zone in the Spare Bedroom, containing let-down bed, wash basin and storage

The bathroom includes further concealed cupboards

The Nursery

The Nursery is spanned by two channelled concrete beams on the line of the columns which provide tracks for the folding partitions. One partition has been removed and the other semi-permanently fixed. At each end the children's beds were fitted into recesses between the party walls of the house with cupboards beside them. The bed recess was later formed into further cupboards. The nanny's bed folded away by day into a cupboard which takes space from the landing, allowing also for a small broom cupboard. Over the doors a continuous range of lockers made full use of the storage potential.

As first completed, the separate parts of the Nursery were distinguished by the colours yellow, Wedgwood blue, white and red ochre. One wall at each end was left in natural grey plaster for each child to draw on. Peter Goldfinger remembers carving a hammer and sickle in the plaster.

Ernö Goldfinger had considerable experience designing furniture and exhibition displays for Paul and Marjorie Abbatt, the leading progressive manufacturers of children's toys and equipment. The Nursery originally had miniature versions of the tubular steel chairs in the Dining Room and of the 'Safari' chairs in the Studio and Living Room. Liz Goldfinger's doll's-house was designed by her father as a modern holiday bungalow in plywood.

The Nursery in 1940. The 1930s ideal of a children's playroom – sunlight, space and self-expression with miniature versions of adult toys

In acquiring 2 Willow Road, the National Trust gratefully acknowledges major grants and donations from the National Heritage Memorial Fund, the Headley Trust, the 20th-Century Society, the Bequest of Harry Walter Fletcher, and National Trust Centres and Associations. Three important works of art have been acquired thanks to donations from the Henry Moore Foundation, the Elephant Trust and the Rayne Foundation. The cinema and film about Willow Road for visitors have been made possible through a donation from the John Ellerman Foundation and a grant from the Arts Council Lottery Fund.

Additional funds are still needed to purchase a sculpture for the garden to replace the Henry Moore that stood there for much of the Goldfingers' time in the house. Donations are welcome and should be addressed to:

2 Willow Road Appeal
The National Trust
Heelis
Kemble Drive
Swindon SN2 2NA

(*Front cover*) 2 Willow Road at night, 1992

(*Back cover*) The spiral stairs with rope balustrade

(*Inside front cover*) Child's alphabet playtray designed by Ernö Goldfinger for Paul and Marjorie Abbatt in the 1930s

(*Title-page*) View from the house in the 1970s, with Henry Moore's elm *Head* (1937) and wooden implements

Photographs: © The Eileen Agar Estate p. 8 (left); photographs by Dell and Wainwright courtesy of *Architectural Review* pp.15 (above right), 16 (above left), 18, 19 (left and above and below right), 20 (above left and below right), 21 (left and right), 25, 26 (above left), 29 (above left), 32; RIBA Library Drawings Collection pp.5 (left), 11 (below right), 12 (below), 15 (above left), 16 (below left and right), 20 (below left), 23 (above), 27 (above); Goldfinger archive pp. 2, 3 (above and below), 4 (right), 5 (right), 8 (right), 9, 12 (above left), 13, 14–15, 14 (above), 17 (left and right); Hulton Deutsch p.10; © The André Kertész Estate p. 6 (right); © The Man Ray Trust/ADAGP, Paris, and DACS, London, 1996 p. 4 (left); © The Henry Moore Foundation p.11 (above right); National Trust Photographic Library/John Bethell pp.1, 26 (below left); NTPL/Dennis Gilbert inside front cover, pp. 7 (below), 22 (above and below left and right), 23 (below), 24, 26 (below right), 27 (below), 28, 29 (above), 30 (below left and right), 31 (left and right), back cover; NTPL/John Hammond p. 29 (below); NTPL/Richard Holttum p.7 (above right); NTPL/Angelo Hornak front cover; © The Roland Penrose Estate 1984 p.11 (left); © SPADEM/ADAGP, Paris, and DACS, London, 1996 pp. 6 (left), 7 (below right).

© 1996 The National Trust Registered charity no. 205846
ISBN 978-1-84359-125-2
Revised 2004, 2008
Published by the National Trust (Enterprises) Ltd

Designed by Rose-Innes Associates

Printed by Heanorgate
for National Trust (Enterprises) Ltd, Heelis, Kemble Drive, Swindon, Wilts SN2 2NA

ISBN 978-1-84359-125-2

9 781843 591252 >